HOW TO BE A BETTER PARTNER
A BRIEF ILLUSTRATED GUIDE FOR DADS

BY
DR. ROBERT ZEITLIN

ILLUSTRATED BY

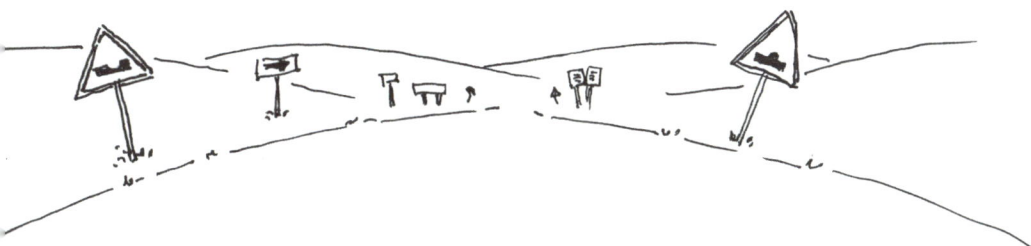

THE RELUCTANT ILLUSTRATOR

To the Love of My Life, Betsy,
who is the strongest person I know.

No better job than being a dad, and no better way to be great at it than learning and re-learning how to be a better spouse. So hard and so good!

David B.

Sharing my "magic beans" is an idea that I've really taken to heart by trying to take the "small, doable tasks" like taking out the trash and doing dishes off my wife's plate. I want to try and be as much of a partner with her as possible which helps alleviate stress in her life. This has definitely helped our relationship and my wife feeling like we're a team. It shows her that I care to help and that I'm curious.

Anthony D.

Absolutely stunning!

It's a quick read, digestible, and perfect for the busy parent who wants to be a better partner and create a solid foundation for their family.

Can everyone read this primer? Having benefited personally from your insight, wisdom, and counsel, I can attest to the impact of your advice.

Margo A.

PREFACE

I acknowledge that my experience is filtered through my perspective as a white, straight, cisgender father and husband. Still, I wrote this book with the intention to support queer dads, straight dads, trans dads, dads of color, and parents who don't conform to the male-female gender binary. I believe that the insights I share here can apply to most couples, even co-parents. When I talk about my life I use gendered terms but, otherwise, I use they/them/their pronouns to include the lived experiences of all readers.

INTRODUCTION

After decades of being a father and over 10 years of writing about parenting, I still feel vulnerable when I wade into a space where men don't often show up. I feel comfortable walking into a hardware store but I stick out in a yoga studio.

If you are curious about parenting and expanding your role in your family, I know how easy it is to feel embarrassed and frustrated. I know how frequently shame is used to shape what we do and don't dare to do.

I applaud you for wading in. You are welcome here.

I am here to support you for one simple reason: our children are the heroes we will need to survive a volatile, uncertain, complex, and ambiguous future. I am the proud father of two amazing grown kids and I am reaching out to my fellow dads because we hold a huge amount of influence in how our kids are raised and how our families function. We can make things worse, even just in our absence. With a few shifts in your mindset and your actions, you also have the power to make things much better.

I have worked with kids and their families for over 20 years in schools, in my practice, and with nonprofits. I have also had the privilege to facilitate thousands of conversations between partners and between kids and their parents. As the dedicated, imperfect husband to the Love of My Life for the last 30+ years, I am offering you the biggest lessons that I have used to maintain and grow our bond.

I am offering you 9 tools to step up for your family. My personal and professional mission to support parents has taught me that your two most important jobs are being a better person and creating a solid relationship with the person with whom you are raising your kids. That's why many of these tips focus on your partner relationship and becoming a better "you."

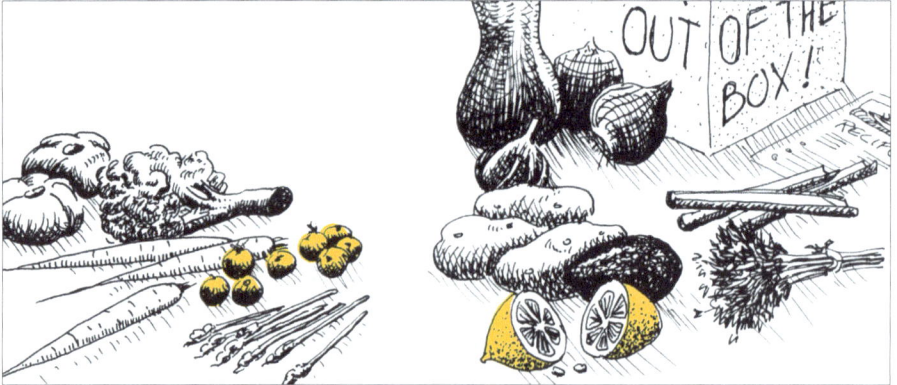

GRAB & GO

I've organized this book so that you can read these first three ideas like you would pick up a soda and bag of chips from your local grab-and-go market. Grab & Go is quick and easy, but don't be fooled! These hacks have been game-changers for the fathers I have coached:

- Ask in the morning (that's when you get a "yes")
- Love languages
- Share your magic beans

THE MEAL KIT

If you don't want to go any deeper, you can stop after Grab & Go, lose the book under the bed, and hope you never need to reopen it. However, if you want to take your partnership to the next level, let's get cooking! Use these next three ideas like a meal kit to make your mark in the kitchen. Here are three ways to show up in a new way for your kids and your partner:

- Co-create agreements (and stop toiling under expectations)
- Learn to meditate
- Expand your Emotional Literacy

COOKING WITH CONFIDENCE

Now you are ready to be The Chef, with the confidence to take on larger challenges in your parenting and partnering. Embracing the wisdom in these last three ideas can shift who you are being in your relationship and in every aspect of your life. These tools enable you to change your life from the inside out, create a stronger parenting unit, and establish the family culture that your rockstar kids deserve!

- DO less
- Pause and Pivot
- BE more

GRAB & GO

SHORT & SWEET TIPS THAT PACK GREAT NUTRITIOUS VALUE

ASK IN THE MORNING

If you ever find yourself in jail and they ask you when you want to schedule your parole review, choose a slot in the morning. Statistically, you are more likely to get released from jail when your parole hearing is in the morning; later in the day, you tend to get a "no" *(Danziger & Levav, 2011).*

What does this have to do with parenting? Adulting means making a ton of decisions every day. With a limited amount of decision-making energy, a stressful workday or your kids asking a million questions is all it takes to use up your reserve.

Although it is easier to answer "no" to questions like "Honey, can I ghost on you and the kids all day Saturday to play golf?" it usually takes more energy to say "yes."

WHEN ARE YOU MOST LIKELY TO GET A "YES"?

If it's late in the day and you want a yes, hold your request for the morning. Approach your partner when they have a full tank of decision-making energy.

Don't approach your partner when they are driving on fumes...
You just set yourself up for a no.

LOVE LANGUAGES

It is easy to assume that everyone likes what you like. Really, though, you form your preferences from your own life experiences. We also tend to choose partners with a different set of experiences, who complement us in some important way. Therefore, the way you feel appreciated and loved is probably not the same as your partner.

DO YOU KNOW WHAT MAKES YOU FEEL LOVED?

The pastor Gary Chapman created the concept of "love languages" 30 years ago. In his hugely popular book The 5 Love Languages, Chapman proposed that our preferences usually fall into five categories:

- **acts of service:** providing some action your partner appreciates.

- **words of affirmation:** encouraging statements that make your partner feel valued.

- **quality time:** designating time with your partner to do what they like.

- **receiving gifts:** buying your partner something they might enjoy.

- **physical touch:** can be a firm back rub or a gentle caress that causes chills.

If my love language is "words of affirmation" and my partner's is "receiving gifts," it would be easy for me to assume that I'd show them how much I love them by writing a heartfelt letter. But since it's not about me, giving my partner a thoughtful present will show them how much I care, because it is in their own "language."

Bottom line: If you learn each other's love language, you will communicate more effectively with your partner.

SHARE YOUR MAGIC BEANS

Even though most of our families rely on two incomes, one person in each relationship (often the woman in a heterosexual marriage) usually wears more hats. Whether it's maintaining the house, shepherding the kids, or remembering the pediatrician's number, their mental load may be greater than you realize.

Looking back, my biggest regret is that I did very little to lighten my wife's mental (and emotional) load while we were raising our kids. I had no idea how much of a burden she carried at the time. I did very little to reduce her having to always remember everything, the invisible labor that burns out many working moms.

Sure, I did take on some household responsibilities over the years, but I only did so when she asked again and again. It took a ton of convincing just to get me to agree to do the laundry or to take over the trash and recycling.

Then, even after I agreed (ugh, this is hard to write), I didn't take true responsibility. I still needed reminders and left my wife with the invisible labor of remembering.

I have always had more flexibility and freedom than my wife did, giving me the power to make a huge difference with little effort. It's like I was handed a bag of magic beans.

Sharing a few of your beans may take some effort, but the impact is huge. It's one little thing to you; it's the million-and-first thing to them.

Start by showing that you are willing to take on a small, doable task. Take on something you can handle every week. When you are ready, here are three steps to take on a small piece of your partner's mental load:

1. Make an offer. Don't wait to be asked.
2. It's about completion. Don't put one dish away and wait for applause.
3. When you take responsibility, do it 100%. Start to finish, AND clean it up.

The invisible labor that weighs your spouse down is having to remember. Focus on the goal: take the need to remember one thing off their plate.

While your partner may be burning themselves out, you may be sitting on a reserve of time and energy that could be used to help them. Think about giving up a little bit of that precious time... and make sure you don't half-ass it!

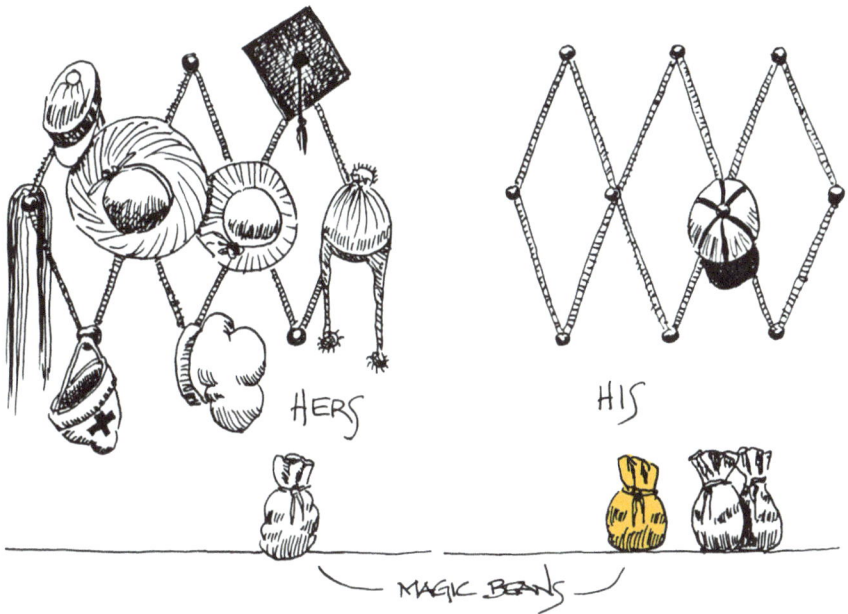

HERS   HIS

MAGIC BEANS

INTERLUDE

As I said earlier, you can take these three Grab & Go ideas and run with them. You don't NEED to read further. But... if you are ready to take on the challenge to raise your parenting and partnering game, read on!

THE MEAL KIT

INVEST IN YOUR DAILY SKILLS TO STABILIZE AND
STRENGTHEN YOUR PARTNERSHIP

CO-CREATE AGREEMENTS

Agreements work better than expectations.

Holding expectations over someone can quickly move your relationship in the wrong direction. Your inner "brat" may cross their arms as if to say, "You're not the boss of me!" Expectations can build resentment and reduce your eagerness to do the things you are told to do.

To explain the difference, I will borrow from Master Coach Steve Chandler:

"Here's the funny thing about human beings. Human beings will love to keep an agreement that they co-authored with you. So if you sit down and you work with someone, and ask them what you can count on, and allow them to ask you for the help they need from you to be able to make the promise, wonderful things happen."

Chandler points out that agreements take two people "creating and recreating, and negotiating and designing together."

When you build the capacity to create empowering agreements WITH your partner (and children!), you are planting a sapling. With consistent attention, water the sapling and watch it grow over the years into a beautiful tree!

In my experience working with families for the last 20 years, agreements open a channel for communication and set up an emotional bank account that will soon be overflowing with trust.

LEARN TO MEDITATE

You are being a lot of things to a lot of people. You need to treat yourself better. Your time and energy are too important. So, let's start with something that can make a real difference.

Imagine you woke up to a science fiction movie where flying cars filled the sky overhead. You can't afford to keep peddling your 10-speed. If I offer you a jet pack, you can get back into the game.

You keep hearing about meditation. I know it may feel like a big step. Wherever you start is great. Insight Timer is a great app with lots of choices. Ziva Meditation (where I learned) has a terrific online program that will get you up to speed in two weeks. You can also commit to spending five or ten minutes in your afternoon doing nothing, just spacing out.

There are a lot of reasons that I recommend you find a meditation practice that works for you and commit to it. For instance, when I meditated this morning (just now), I practiced:

- holding the internal boundary that anything I thought or felt could wait for 20 minutes.

- compassion for myself as my mind wandered and I gently shepherded it back using my mantra.

- the humor to laugh at myself for being so dramatic about how hard this is.

- gratitude to myself for committing to this practice, even though the benefits are hard to see in the short term.

- tolerance for the frustration that I am feeling while I practice patience, gratitude, and compassion, and strengthen my internal boundaries.

These are the benefits I get from the meditation I do each day. By practicing daily, I also get stress relief, copious amounts of rest, and I raise my internal level of peace.

Your brain needs a break from focusing every minute of the day. It's exhausting to have to focus on a million things from the moment you wake up until you fall asleep at night, keeping your eye on the ball, being on time, listening actively, and fighting the urge to drift off or procrastinate.

You can't make good decisions if you don't refuel. At some point, you need to give yourself a "time out." Tell yourself, "You just sit there for a minute until you can slow down."

Learning to meditate is an investment we need to make in our families. I know that meditating is a big step but it is a small move in the larger scheme of what your brain and relationships need.

EXPAND YOUR EMOTIONAL LITERACY

When I called him to complain about my day, my friend Charles asked me, "Are you having a bad day or a bad five minutes?"

I'm so glad that I called him. I didn't realize that I could pause and let this set of feelings pass through me.

It's a cruel joke: feeling bad can isolate you, keeping you away from those who can help you feel better. Especially if you are socialized to blow up and/or run away. Yes, guys. If you were socialized as male, I'm looking at you.

When a feeling arises that doesn't sit well with you, Joan Rosenberg has some good news: that bad mood doesn't need to ruin your day. You can limit an "unpleasant emotion" to 90 seconds of feeling uncomfortable.

The unpleasant feelings that we often work hard to avoid are sadness, shame, anger, helplessness, vulnerability, embarrassment, guilt, disappointment, and frustration (I added guilt to Rosenberg's list).

Instead of getting carried away by some story about how that kid in 3rd grade made fun of you (you can fill in the rest), you can snap out of that flashback by learning to identify and name the unpleasant feeling that triggered you.

Rosenberg's approach: rather than spending your evening FEELING helpless, identify the fact THAT you are feeling helpless.

When you learn to identify these unpleasant feelings, you interrupt a hijacking: the discomfort that hijacks your limbic system, floods you with hormones, and can trigger your fight-or-flight nervous system. But… when you learn how to identify the feelings, you can set a timer and let those feelings come and go. The hijacking of your body only lasts for about 90 seconds.

Practicing Rosenberg's formula to identify your feelings is the first step to growing your Emotional Intelligence. For instance, when you only have a few minutes to work through the day's events with your partner, identifying what feelings you experienced will allow you each to connect more deeply. You will be surprised how your relationship improves when you expand your vocabulary!

INTERLUDE

Now that you have learned how meditation can increase your emotional and relational intelligence and you have glimpsed the power of co-creating agreements rather than holding expectations, you are ready for three high-level insights that can take you, your partnership, and your family to new heights.

Warning: a funny thing might start happening as you integrate these next three ideas into your life. People around you might start to notice that something has changed in you, even if they don't know what it is. You may get questions like, "Are you doing something different?" or "Did you change your hair?"

COOKING WITH CONFIDENCE

HIGH-IMPACT MOVES THAT WILL TRANSFORM
HOW YOU SHOW UP FOR YOUR FAMILY

DO LESS

Every single force in the world (schools, experts, Instagram, your relatives) is in on the scam to make you feel like you are doing too little.

You aren't only raising a child. You prepare dinners that need to prevent colon cancer. You study how to pave the road to your kid's Ivy League education.

Face it: before you get out of bed in the morning, you hoist the weight of the world on your shoulders. As a parent, you are told that your job is to save the universe.

It's a lose-lose proposition. Get up early to prepare the perfect, organic, gluten-free, Instagram-ready lunch then... open your email to read another article telling you how you are doing it all wrong.

HOW DO YOU HANDLE ALL OF THAT PRESSURE?

Parenting has become a no-win profession. This is a recipe for stressed-out parents AND stressed-out kids.

I am on the front line of this stress epidemic. I have been privileged to help thousands of parents and kids communicate about the things that matter the most: pressure, expectations, and risky behavior.

I respect what you are doing. I have a suggestion, from one parent to another:

DOWNSHIFT.

I am pulling out a post-it and scribbling you a BIG ASS PERMISSION SLIP (hat tip to Coach Amy E. Smith).

You now have my permission, as a Licensed Psychologist and a parent who has been there to...

DO. A. LITTLE. LESS.

Your kids need you to be centered and calm and in control. Let them run around for a change. Press PAUSE on the chasing and the yelling.

HERE ARE THREE IDEAS TO GET YOU STARTED:

1) FORGIVE YOURSELF

Let's start with a BIG ASS PERMISSION SLIP to forgive yourself for being an imperfect parent. If you are like me, you had zero training. I also wasn't always paying attention from birth to 18 when I had my best chance to observe real parents at work.

While you're at it, here's an extra BIG ASS PERMISSION SLIP for your partner. They are doing the best they can. They may seem like they don't care to learn more. They may be stubborn. But really, like most of us, they are scared that they are royally screwing it up. All the time. Give them a break.

2) BACK AWAY FROM THE SAW BLADE

You can't keep going at this pace. You can't be productive if you always go-go-go and never breathe or hydrate. You need to sharpen the saw (a la Stephen Covey). You need to carve out time to take care of yourself.

When you do it for the first time, you will see a HUGE difference in your attitude as a parent. You will wonder "Why didn't I do this before?"

When you make the commitment to yourself to step back, you will start to see the difference in your kids.

3) MISTAKES = LEARNING

My last BIG ASS PERMISSION SLIP is for you to give to your kids. Take a moment to reflect on how many successes and failures got you to this point in your life. Now try to subtract the failures from the picture. Would you be who you are? I wouldn't. The biggest turning points in my life came from tragedy and mishap. I wouldn't trade them for the world.

Give your kids permission to stray from the path. A lot of learning can happen when we shut up, stop structuring everything, and choose to stop filling their little heads with knowledge. Let them be imperfect learners. Ease up on the desire to control everything they get, do, and see.

BONUS PRO TIP

If you want more ideas to help with your kids' learning, check out my pandemic-inspired book *"But I'm Not a Teacher! A Parent's Guide to Learning Under Lockdown."*

PAUSE AND PIVOT

"Quitting requires being okay with not knowing what might have been"

from "Quit" by Annie Duke (2022)

I coach parents to practice strategic quitting rather than wasting energy playing out scripts that we were handed.

Maybe playing the part of working mom or breadwinner doesn't fit you. If your story is burning you out, you can choose to write a new one.

Before you can pivot, you need to slow down. As leaders of our families, we can pump the brakes by applying the business concept of strategic quitting.

HOW TO QUIT, STRATEGICALLY

Learning how to quit what isn't working frees your time and energy for what really matters.

What really matters to you? Making a lot of money, fame and fortune, or leaving a legacy? None of it will happen without the ability to quit what isn't working.

Quitting is about choice, taking control, and being the driver of your own life. I know quitting has a bad rap. We feel like we should persist and outwork expectations. That way, no one can criticize us. These goals are exhausting... and overrated!

The biggest difference between a professional poker player and an amateur is that the pro knows when to fold so they can win big later.

LOSE

KEEP!

WooHoo!

Think of that conversation with the long-winded friend who you should have cut off 30 minutes ago. You love them but you are never going to get that half hour back. Now you have less time for the gym.

How long have you been trying to carve out just an hour a week to start that book, to get that project going, or to learn about meditating? If you could quit the stuff that doesn't honor your goals, you could find an hour or more.

The most powerful example of quitting comes from a study of those who lost their lives battling forest fires:

Twenty-three firefighters who died in the 1990s in the Western U.S. could have survived if they had done one thing: drop their tools.

If they had only chosen to drop their chainsaws and packs, shedding the extra weight, they would have added distance to each footfall and could have escaped the fire that consumed them.

University of Michigan Professor of Organizational Behavior and Psychology Karl E. Weick learned that some firefighters didn't drop their tools because they saw their chainsaws and axes as extensions of themselves. The 23 firefighters died because they could not shift their mindset from I-am-someone-who-fights-fires to I-am-someone-who-needs-to-run-for-my-life. Their identity weighed them down.

How might this example apply to your life?

Imagine that time when a feeling drove you to act. Maybe you had unfinished business that made it harder to respond to who and what was actually in front of you at that moment.

Learning to drop your tools will allow you to fully experience what lies down the new path that the world offers you. What do you need to drop your tools and pivot?

- What signal are you waiting for?
- Would you read the signal accurately?
- Would you react in time, pivoting smoothly from one direction to the next?

BE MORE

What do I mean by Be More?

Master coach Devon Bandison helped me see the relationship between DO-ing, BE-ing, and HAVE-ing:

We are always doing. Most of what we do is often in the service of having and getting things. We leave who we are BE-ing in last place, only as a by-product of the DO-ing and the HAVE-ing.

Sometimes we let doing drive our lives because it's hard to figure out who we are and who we are becoming. But you are a human being, not a human doing.

Devon suggested that we can lead a more intentional life by changing the order from DO-HAVE-BE to BE-DO-HAVE. Placing BE-ing first gives our identity the power to drive what we do and attain.

For instance, it is irrational to attribute our status at home to our doing. Who we are being is much more important to our kids and our families.

You may feel like you are on a treadmill chasing something that you lack. You may feel stuck until you can get that promotion or house. You need money or a degree or a car or healthcare. You ask yourself:

- Who am I if I quit my job?
- How will I ever face my partner if I lose that promotion?
- Who am I if I'm not the Fun Dad?

If these questions run your life, your actions show who you are: busy, stressed, ineffective, and helpless to change anything.

Asking yourself, "Who am I if I am not doing what I'm doing?" is the first step to stopping DO-ing from defining who you are BE-ing.

How do you make the shift from doing to being? – Flip the script:

- choose how and where and on whom to spend your time.
- take action on purpose.
- get your behavior to follow your roadmap.

Figure out who you want to become and watch your actions get in line behind you.

Jim Rohn said, "Learn to work harder on yourself than you do on your job. If you work hard on your job you can make a living, but if you work hard on yourself you'll make a fortune."

In other words, "BE more than DO." Sometimes your kids will be better served when you choose to "do nothing." Stepping back from the problem can give your child the space to innovate and learn something in the process.

Then you can move on to the more important questions:

- Could I actually be a writer?
- What if I decide to love my body as it is today?
- Would the world accept me as a professional bagpiper?

CONCLUSION

Who are you BE-ing? Who are you BE-ing that person FOR?

If you take one idea from this short book and choose to act on it for the next 30 days, who will you BE then?

Your actions vote for the person you are. Learn how to drop your tools, pivot, and quit strategically to vote for the person who you want to be and that your kids deserve.

REQUEST FOR FEEDBACK

Dear Reader, I hope you enjoyed this guide for Dads. Whether you are a father or not, I would love to know:

- What's one thing from this book you would try?
- What's one topic that you'd like to learn more about?

If you have a minute to leave a comment with answers to these questions on my website, I would be very grateful!
www.robertzeitlin.com

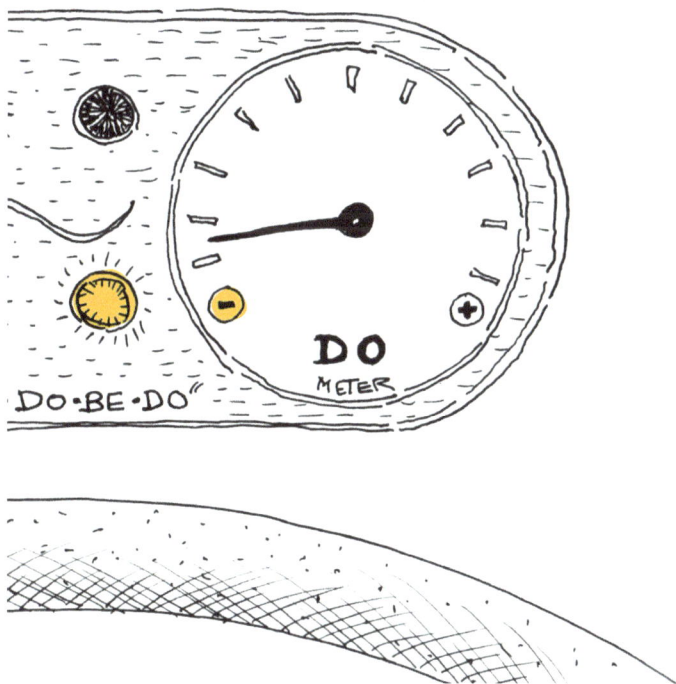

DO·BE·DO

DO METER

REFERENCES AND FURTHER READING

Chapman, G. (2015). The 5 love languages: The secret to love that lasts. Northfield Publishing.

Covey, S. R. (2022). The 7 Habits of Highly Effective Families (fully revised and updated): Creating a nurturing family in a turbulent world. Golden Press.

Danziger, S. & Levav, J. (2011). "Extraneous factors in judicial decisions," in Proceedings of the National Academy of Science, February 2011.

Dearly, V. (2022). How to do hard things: Actual real-life advice on friends, love, career, well-being, mindset, and more. DK Publishing.

Donovan, D. (2023). The anti-planner: How to get sh*t done when you don't feel like it. Anti-Boring Books.

Duke, A. (2022). Quit! The power of knowing when to walk away. Portfolio.

Ehlers, E. (2021). Hope is a verb: Six steps to radical optimism when the world seems broken. Andrews McMeel.

Greene, M. & Bava, S. (2018). The relational book for parenting: Raising children to connect, collaborate, and innovate by growing our families' relationship. CreateSpace.

Heller, E. (2022). Kids super journal: Mindfulness + journaling = super journaling. Pig and Whale.

Loehnen, E. (2023). On our best behavior: The seven deadly sins and the price women pay to be good. The Dial Press.

Rosenberg, J. L. (2019). 90 Seconds to a life you love: How to master your difficult feelings to cultivate lasting confidence, resilience, and authenticity. Little Brown.

Weick, K. E. (2007). "Drop your tools: On reconfiguring management education," in Journal of Management Education, vol. 31, no. 1, pages 5-16, February 2007.

Zeitlin, R. (2020). But I'm not a teacher! A parent's guide to learning under lockdown. Haverford, PA: Robert Zeitlin.

Zeitlin, R. (2020). Laugh more, yell less. A guide to raising kick-ass kids. Stuck-at-home edition. Haverford, PA: Robert Zeitlin.

AKNOWLEDGEMENTS

My deepest gratitude is for Betsy, whose love endures through thick and thin, and who holds space for me to be the kind, conscientious, and compassionate partner I can be. I could not do this work without her support and the love of my family: our kids Lilly and Ian, my sisters Lisagail and Karen, my in-laws Sally and Mo, and my parents Lynn and Gary, both of blessed memory.

Thanks to my Support Team for helping me to get through every week: Charles Grove, Jessica Anwyl, Nate Turner, Danny Cramer, and Kiki Wilkinson. Heather Foster, Katie Schultz, Elyss Gregory, Vicki Livolsi, and Dawn Martesi are new additions to the Team that made me feel welcome and loved (yes, loved at a day job!), giving me the energy to write this book and continue this important work. Thanks also to my incredibly talented and empathetic professional support team, Angela Claire Howard, Ruthy Kaiser, and Amber Shirley.

Finally, I need to express my gratitude for Brainstorm Road (BSR), the creative playground that provided the feedback and support I needed to write this book. This beautiful community was designed by Margo Aaron and Kristin Hatcher and is managed with grace by the one and only Rick Kitigawa. I found my fiercest advocates on The Road: Courtney, Marta, Foxy, Rishma, Doug, and the aforementioned Margo and Rick. BSR is also where I met my inimitable illustrator and Ambassadors Diane, Carolina, Heat, and Erin.

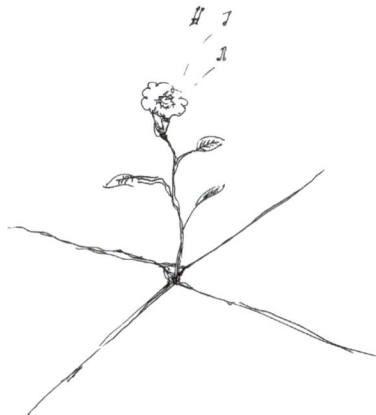

CREDITS

DR. ROBERT ZEITLIN

Dr. Robert Zeitlin is a Positive Psychologist and Feminist Dad who coaches other fathers across the country and world from his offices in Philadelphia, PA.

From Dr. Zeitlin: "For over 30 years, before she was pregnant with our first child, I have worked with my wife to maintain a warm and joyful family culture. We manage imbalances in our workloads, share childcare responsibilities, and negotiate how to each get our needs met.

As a licensed psychologist and the happily married (for 30+ years) father of two kick-ass (now grown) kids, I have combined my experience with my training to help parents create the families their kids deserve. I coach parents to improve their partnerships and parenting styles.

In addition to my private practice, I have worked in schools for 20+ years, consulting with teachers and parents on children's behavior and learning. I have created and run dozens of workshops, published books and a podcast, and love speaking to parent groups."

THE RELUCTANT ILLUSTRATOR

Illustrations and Book Design: The Reluctant Illustrator draws from reflections, observations and musings about self, culture and the human condition. Made with a skewed glance and a wandering hand, simple pen and ink drawings depict the curious ways we relate to and engage the world with our teetering, two-legged, wobbly balance.

thereluctantillustrator.com

www.ingramcontent.com/pod-product-compliance
Lightning Source LLC
Chambersburg PA
CBHW041105110426
42740CB00043B/155